Piano Music for Little Fingers

Book 2

Ann Patrick Green

Dover Publications, Inc.
Mineola, New York

Bibliographical Note

Piano Music for Little Fingers—Book 2 is a new work, first published by Dover Publications, Inc., in 2012.

The copyrighted Family Circus characters by Bil Keane appear with permission granted by the Bil Keane family and may not be copied or reproduced in any form for any purpose without the express written authorization of the Bil Keane family.

International Standard Book Number

ISBN-13: 978-0-486-48825-7
ISBN-10: 0-486-48825-X

Manufactured in the United States by Courier Corporation
48825X01
www.doverpublications.com